Love

Fear

Reality

SPOKENVERB

Copyright © 2019 by Joel Martin (A.K.A. Spoken Verb)

All rights reserved. This book or parts thereof may not be reproduced in any form, stored in any retrieval system, or transmitted in any form by any means—electronic, mechanical, photocopy, recording, or otherwise—without prior written permission of the publisher, except as provided by United States of America copyright law or for the use of brief quotations in a book review.

ISBN 978-0-578-61218-8

RepYahOn Publishing

Chattanooga, TN

Dedication

This book is dedicated to the lost sheep going thru the curses of Deuteronomy 28:15-68. Remember who you are and who chose you and Repent. Much love

Thank you

I want to thank Jehovah God (Psalm 83:18), because without Your blessings, none of this would be possible. As Proverbs 10:22 states, "It is the blessing of Jehovah that makes one rich, and He adds no pain with it" (NWT)

I also want to thank my mom Alisa Kendrick, my brother Jarrett Martin, my sister Tamara Kendrick and my niece Jada and nephew Mekhai for sticking beside me and bringing comfort to me during my darkest hour. I will forever be grateful, and I Love You. I also would like to recognize the Martin Family and the Elder Family. I love you, as well.

A special thanks to Coach Laura Brown, my mentor on this publishing journey. You were truly a blessing.

About the Author

Spoken Verb, a.k.a. Joel Martin, is an author, spoken word artist, and the owner and CEO of RepYahOn, a clothing lifestyle brand created to encourage positivity and self-love.

Joel was born in Chattanooga TN and introduced to the street life at the age of sixteen. He was book smart and street smart. A combination that helped him maneuver through the city of Indianapolis IN. Where he moved to when he was 17 years old. Being raised as a Jehovah's Witness, he also had a sense of spirituality, which helped to develop his conscious and a thirst for knowledge.

He attended Clark Atlanta University until his senior year when he left to make his mark on the Atlanta music scene, along with his younger brother. he was ready to "ball or die."

He enjoys listening to music or reading books, particularly the Bible. He is a lover of poetry, music, art, women, animals, the beach, and above all, God, family, and friends. This is his first book of poetry, and hopefully not his last.

Connect with SpokenVerb

To request SpokenVerb for performances, contact him at:

- Email: joelpmartinis@gmail.com
- Instagram - @Repyahon
- Facebook - www.facebook.com/mrTouche

To view RepYahOn Lifestyle Brand go to www.howdoyafeel.com.

Contents

- About the Author 5
- Love 9
  - Unanswered Prayer 10
  - Wo – Bot 13
  - Online Affair 15
  - Love on a 2-way Street 18
  - How Do You Communicate Passion? 22
- Fear 25
  - I Give Up 26
  - Tears of a Clown 28
  - A Soldier's Story 30
  - Voices 31
- Reality 35
  - Can You Walk on Water? 36
  - Unreal Reality 38
  - CHATTANOOGA 41
  - Lost Tribes 47

Love

Unanswered Prayer

One day while meditating

Alright... I was smoking weed

I decided to remind God

Just in case He might've forgot

To send me the perfect woman

Whether she was created or not

Not realizing the importance of this chance I had

I almost blew my chance

By simply asking for Halle Berry's face and

Jennifer Lopez's ass

But then I dreamed of her, every night

Just like, when I was younger

The dream was live in color

My visions became more clear

It was like she was already here

It seemed so real

So, I asked

Let her be brown skin, honey brown

So I can taste it on her lips

Let her have pretty eyes and an attractive smile

PLEASE GOD, let her have all her teeth

Let her laugh at all my jokes because she enjoys hearing it from me

Let her not be addicted,

Have to take any prescriptions

A vibrant thing, spiritual

Let her have enjoyed life some, with no children

But even if she did, let it just be one

Let her baby dad live in another state

Far, far away

So he don't come by her house

Talking 'bout

Where my kid at because he sees my car in her driveway

Let her parents treat me like fam
Especially her Pops
Let him understand, that she's in good hands
Because she finally found a good man
And all these things I ask and pray
In Your Son's name
Oh yea, God, before I let it end
Lookout for my lil' brother
Let this perfect woman have a twin
Amen

Wo - Bot

Artificial intelligence

Yet so realistic

Looks like an angel from Heaven

But she's electric

Like city lights

A product of the city life

Dat sparkle in her eyes

Is because her soul is made from conflict diamonds

She says turn me on

Press play

And we can do whatever on the first date

I give her what it takes

She gives me what my will is

Her heart is Japanese

Her booty is Brazilian

Her love is digital

Even wireless

So when she's running low

Then I plug it in

She's my gravity

Cause she holds me down

Her love's protected by viper

When I'm not around

She says turn me on

Press play

And we can do whatever on the first date

I give her what it takes

She gives me what my will is

Her heart is Japanese

Her booty is Brazilian

Online Affair

She lets her eyes hold the whole conversation

Patiently waiting, anticipating on me to say something like

Hello, Hi, or Hey. It's been a long time or

YOU ARE MY SOULMATE!

Could it be that...

Sparkle in your eyes

That makes me wonder,

Are you the essence of the sunshine

Or is your soul made of diamonds

Wondering...

Is your heart of gold

It gotta be...

Because you're so fine, so sexy, so young, so beautiful.

I know you heard it before

But you deserve to be told.

Your silence...

Tells me you must be contemplating,

The idea of leaving your man stuck home aggravated

To come be with me,

And if he's like, "where you going baby?"

Tell him don't be alarmed

Read the signs

Because in my arms is where you want to be.

Can I... make all your senses come alive

Not just physically but mentally, spiritually

So that every time, you look at me

With hypnotized eyes

It's like our souls combined online

SO. BE. MINE...

If only for one night, at a time

Let me feel your presence in my sleep

While you dream of how it would be

For me, to taste your sweet and sticky spot,

Until your knees get weak and your body gets hot

Then tell me,

When can we meet?

Love on a 2-way Street

Do you believe in love at first sight?

Well neither did I

Then I met her, and I opened my eyes

Seen past the lust

Into the future existence of us

And my heart was thrown off guard

By this beautiful pattern interrupt

Some say your heart skips a beat

Mine was ready to leap in her chest

All that I am is yours for just a kiss

Never have I met a woman like this free spirit

Smokes Kush

Gets high enough to skydive from airplanes.

Spends snow days busting rounds in a shooting range

The average guy she would intimidate
But I found her easy to entertain
Our cars are the same
Certain phrases we would say were the same
I thought we were on the same page
Barnes and Noble was our first date
Never before have I met a woman
I wanted to give my last name
Well maybe once but she don't really count
Because I was young and sprung
Not knowing what love is about
Now the shoe is on the other foot
I'm 32 she's 23

I'm ready to settle down.

She enjoys being free

I now know what it means,

To have found love on a two-way street

When two passersby in life, headed in different directions, meet

The time spent is often brief

And unless one turns around

While the other slows down

How will we know if we were meant to be

Foreva and eva and eva

But I'm too stubborn, and she's so rebellious

And now the further we pull away

The memory of the warm feeling her smile gave me

Begins to fade

Then the space created from the mistake made of moving too late

Can become as great as outer space

Just like Andre 3k say

"Spaceships don't come equipped with rear view mirrors; they dip."[1]

I'm on to the next star

That means there will come a time

When we want to look back and can't

And I don't want to think, I lost my soulmate

Because my heart couldn't communicate with my brain, so my mouth would know what to say

So I decide to write what's on my heart

Before you take it away

---

[1] UGK (2007). International Player's Anthem (I Choose You). On *Underground Kingz*.

How Do You Communicate Passion?

What's the best way to communicate passion

Is it in the way a bird sings or a bee dances

How do you

Tell someone you've just met

You are the memory I want to relive during my last breath?

How do you

Express interest to a complete stranger

Without sounding stranger or lamer

Than the last guy who tried

But got the hand or the middle finger?

How can I tell you

How much I really want you

That you're like the warm feeling from a coastal sunset at summer's end

Fallen graces

So amazing

Just to
Be the rose petals in the center of your Bath and Body Works oasis

Just to
Touch you in a place that will have you thinking of love

Just to
Whisper sweet nothings for your chocolate kisses and hugs

Just to
Slow dance with affection,

Romancing

Fingers caressing

Sending me mental images of you undressing

Just to
Get you loose with enthusiasm

The anticipation got you shaking

Until you orgasm

As I excel...you exhale,

Breathe deep with a sigh

Just to
Be your fountain of love
And fill your cup with the champagne of my thigh
Because I want to see you naked
We can do it wherever
But I realize your presence
Is a far greater pleasure
And I know, its spiritual
When our hands hold
And only good can get better
That's when I looked into her eyes
and seen the other side of forever
So I'm saying
Its natural
The same way a bird sings or a bee dances
Is the way I communicate passion

Fear

I Give Up

I'm sick of women treating me like shit

I think I'm going to be happy alone

But I'm stuck in this world,
and I can't call it quits

Everything that can go wrong has gone wrong So

I'm gone

I give up

Giving up on love

Giving up on happiness

Giving up on everything

When you see me smile, it won't be real

It might seem like

I'm the happiest person in the world,

But it's just the pill

Cause you don't know how I feel,

Really, inside I'm dying,

My heart is crying, and it's broken into a million teeny, tiny pieces

I love, being in love, but I just don't think that

It will happen to me again

I'm not depressed, it's just

This blue undertone, funk, love jones mood that I seem to be in

I'm done looking for love

Love should be looking for me

I give up! YOU WIN!!

Tears of a Clown

Take a look into my eyes

Can you see the pain that they hide?

Because pride can only take you so far

Underestimated all my life

That if I hold it to myself inside

I'll be the one to die from a cold heart.

A world without love is a world without fear

Words spoken from generations of thugs

Bread from blood, sweat, and no tears

With dry eyes

We witness living life from the outside looking in

Because soldiers don't cry

We're supposed to kill or die over respect

Dreaming of my family trying to get by

If Pops became another once a month check

They say that the sun will come out tomorrow

But without a perfect mix of blue and yellow

The end of our man-made rainbow

Will lead to dirt roads on the other side of the ghetto

A Soldier's Story

They say life goes on, still da same

Not for long though, we living in the last days

Lovers of money

Be the first to say they want change

But all they do is pass the blame,

Sit and complain

Give it a name

Call it debate.

And I'll say it to their motherfucking face.

It's the same ones who start the gossip

Be the same ones who killed hip-hop's prophets

Now you wonder why mc's selling out for the profit

Voices

Sometimes I hear voices.

They are a little louder than a conscious

In fact, they are obnoxious

When I'm alone, I'm afraid.

Because in my head

I'm not alone

I'm surrounded by spirits that want me dead.

One tells me

That I ain't shit.

No matter how accomplished I become, that I'll never be shit

So I should just quit

No matter how nice your clothes and cars are,

No matter how large your house or bank account,

No matter how much you try to smile

No one has loved you since you were a child

Another one tells me

I'm gone kill you.

If you smoke that cigarette,

If you have sex with that chick,

If you step outside your house

I'm gone kill you.

And I BELIEVE THEM.

Instantly I began to distance myself from friends

That woman that wanted me

No longer understands.

Business gone; bank account closed

Cars are gone; house foreclosed.

All I have left is my mother
and these nice clothes

And they're both getting old

Then a VOICE tells me

I hear You

I hear your cry for help

You are not by yourself

I am near you

Pray to me

Tell me your fear, your pain, and anxiety

I will take your right hand and make you whole again

I Am who I say I Am.

AND I BELIEVE HIM...

Reality

Can You Walk on Water?

CAN YOU WALK ON WATER?

When you read this, you may call to mind the Bible scripture Matt 14:24-26

It tells the incident of when the disciples were in a boat

Hundreds of yards away from the shore and

They caught sight of Jesus walking on the sea

CAN YOU WALK ON WATER?

Many get discouraged when they stumble, or

Make mistakes because of our imperfect state

And simply want to just give up

God already knows that we are imperfect

He knows that we will fall short and has set in place a ransom (John 3:16) for repentant ones

Jesus being a perfect man,
the Son of Almighty GOD,
anointed with holy spirit
and powers from GOD (Acts 10:38, John 6:29)
set a perfect example of
how we are to serve GOD and show love and kindness toward others

Since we are imperfect humans, we will not be able to serve GOD in the same perfect way as Jesus.

God understands that, He just wants us to put

forth an effort

CAN YOU WALK ON WATER?

The answer is YES

We simply have to freeze it first

Although we are not able to do it exactly how Jesus did

We can still follow his footsteps.

Unreal Reality

As a New Year approaches

It's wintertime but some days are hot and humid

Scientists say the Earth is off its axis

Others say Armageddon is looming

The unaware are unafraid

Still, they sleep uneasy

Tossing and turning like on a broken box spring mattress

Like being awake and still dreaming

Feeling like your soul is restless

Yes... this is the time for repentance

Asking God for blessings or forgiveness,

With no commitments, no strings attached

Like asking to be shown favor, for being born poor and black

Unlikely

So some continue to waste borrowed time away

Not realizing we are closer to a conclusion

Then we were yesterday

Mothers killing their own babies

Fathers molesting the adolescence

False teaching has risen

at an all-time progression

'Cause from the pulpit

Some speak bull shit

AntiChrist

Preachers who promote profit and politics

And in their eyes

WAR is the acronym for We Are Right

So they say we must fight

Until the other side believes

Amidst the chemicals, pistol smoke, and cigarette butts

Makes it hard for kids to breathe.

Please don't be deceived,

Bad association

Is the majority population

Catholicism, Buddhism, Hinduism, Muslim, Christendom

I witness the hypnotism,

Hypocrisy of democracy

Violent pacifist

Went from a crackhead to a Black man for President

And still, no real change has begun

So our Father who art in Heaven

Hallowed be Thy name

Let Your Kingdom come

CHATTANOOGA

I'm from the city of ditches
Full of fiends and killas
Where dope dealers
And grave diggers getting richer
Prominent figures
Politic above city streets
With front row seats
To watch us fight for position
To hustle to eat
Struggle to beat the odds stacked against us
Another day older
Another day closer to God
Please forgive us
Because living hard
Is like a full-time job
I gotta get mine
But my attitude is filthy
I'm 39 feeling like I just turned 50

Young Black and gifted

Some say a genius

Imagine me at 18 trying to be an O.G.

With a scholarship from the NAACP

Because a mind is a terrible thing to waste

They say the grind is a terrible thing to chase

Until you see your mom struggling

With bills to pay

That's why they say

Ain't no hallelujah in Chattanooga

The old carry bibles

While the young tote rugers

One to save ya ass

The other to save ya soul

You can live fast or slow

But you not promised tomorrow

And Baby, that's how it goes

You already know

The end of the rainbow

Is just another dirt road

A perfect mix of blue and yellow

Money Green

Causing catastrophe

Ultraviolet brings violence

Infrared dotted for accuracy

Casualties of war

No remorse on these streets

Because around here

They cutthroat like Cherokee

Warriors

Hitting back streets

Creeping through the shadows

Riding mustang and Camaros

Nickel plated bows

With the hollow tipped arrows

Keeping one eye on the crosshairs
The other on the sparrow
That's why I shoot first
And ask questions last
And if the truth hurts
Baby don't ask
This Chattanooga
Yea this Chattanooga
But don't let em fool ya
It's the powers that be
That want to divide us
Saying Black on Black crime is
The reason we won't prevail
When the system they got in place
Is designed for us to fail
They would rather see us dead or in jail
Locked in a box or a cell

Or on our knees praying

To white Jesus for help

Awaiting on Heaven

But we too scared of death

And the devil using weapons

That got us scared as hell

Like police

Who threaten to arrest us
but kill us without a care

We are sheep without a Shepherd

Ready for revolution

But we really not prepared

We don't farm

we don't hunt

We don't train our kids

How to use a gun

See White folks got militias
And they want us to fight back
With peaceful resistance
What are we going to do
march until they submit
See Martin Luther King's dream
Didn't mean ask for permission
Or wait for the oppressor
To have empathy for the oppressed
But it was a hope
For true equality and pure freedom
Because that can exist
Whether it happens now
Or in the near future
I hope it comes to Chattanooga

Lost Tribes

R.I.P. to Nipsey Hussle

And all the ones that died before you

The ones who fought for the people

And the ones that didn't know how to

The ones caught in a system of lies

Yea because that's what they taught you

Forced upon a generation of lives

By the same people that bought you

Sold...unto your enemies

Who think they own and control us

and the way our ancestors were treated

How can I forget that you owe us

I know you know us

The Bible states in Deuteronomy 28:68

That the Israelites would go back to Egypt on ships

And Egypt is synonymous with bondage

That's why they had iron yokes upon our necks

And because of God's love for his children

Our enemies still look at us as threats

While we want to integrate

They used to look at us as pets

While we were trying to assimilate

All they wanted was free work and sex

While we needed food on our dinner plate

Now if they pay me a little more on my check

I promise I won't riot or demonstrate

See, I know according to the Bible who I am

And that the Devil may offer the worlds riches

But God has a better retirement plan

And that our redemption as a people

won't come from a man

But only when the Son comes to claim his Kingdom come

Amen

See Revelation 2:9 says I know your tribulation

But you are a rich nation

Because it's you who are the children of Abraham, Isaac, and Jacob

And if your pastor won't tell you this

Ask him, why are you playing with my soul.

It's because he is 501-3c

You'll see

That he's aligned with the Devil

But be patient

Your salvation is near

And if you return to His statutes and commandments

all your wounds will be healed

So come back lost tribe come back

So you can be gathered from where you were scattered

Repent lost tribe…

Repentance

Means to turn away from all these sinful man-made traditions

Like Easter, Halloween, and Christmas

Awake lost tribe awaken

To who you were once before

So that you won't be a lost tribe anymore

Connect with SpokenVerb

To request SpokenVerb for performances, contact him at:

- Email: joelpmartinis@gmail.com
- Instagram - @Repyahon
- Facebook- www.facebook.com/mrTouche

To view RepYahon Lifestyle Brand go to www.howdoyafeel.com.

www.ingramcontent.com/pod-product-compliance
Lightning Source LLC
Chambersburg PA
CBHW071416290426
44108CB00014B/1844